Somewhere
In Between
Quilts and Quilters
of Illinois

By
Rita Barrow Barber

American Quilter's Society

P.O. Box 3290 • Paducah, Kentucky 42001

The Quilt

I have the greatest fun at night,
When casement windows are all bright.
I make believe each one's a square
Of some great quilt up in the air.

The blocks of gold have black between,
Wherever only night is seen.
It surely makes a mammoth quilt —
With bits of dark and checks of gilt —
To cover up the tired day
In such a cozy sort of way.

By Mary Effie Lee Newsome
Taken from *Caroling Dusk*,
Harper & Brothers Publishing, NY, 1927

Dedication

To Clara Belle Alltop Milbrad, my maternal grandmother, who always had time to sit on the steps in the sunshine. She made sure there were hot apple dumplings for my lunch. She showed me how to "make it on my hands" and answered my endless questions, even as she asked, "'Deed child, where do you ever come up with so many questions?"

In answer to her question, "I don't know where all the questions come from, Grandma. But I have more now than ever."

Acknowledgements

In addition to all of those mentioned in the text who so generously shared their time, information and quilts, there are others who deserve mention.

A very special thanks to Veronica Fesser who edited my manuscript and who assisted me through the ordeal with unending encouragement.

Special thanks to Dorothy Callahan Christian and Blanche Moye Cook who helped me extensively in their respective sections of the state.

Special thanks to Mary Lou Remling and Iris Zimmer of the Carlinville Library for locating all the literature for me.

For assistance in locating quilts and/or information about quilts and quilters:
    Jill Adsit, Milford, IL
    Cuesta Benberry, St. Louis, MO
    Barbara Brackman, Lawrence, KS
    Pam Campbell, Stearns Technical Textiles
        Company
    Verna Drake, Watseka, IL
    Joyce Gross, Mill Valley, CA
    Amy L. Harris, Art Institute of Chicago
    Alexia Helsley, South Carolina Department of
        Archives and History
    Frank Hoell, R.R. Donnelley & Sons Company
    Olivia Mahoney, Chicago Historical Society
    Darlene Marion, Kankakee County Historical
        Society
    Mary Lou McGinnis, Quincy, IL
    Julie Silber, Oakland, CA
    Terry Suhre, Illinois State Museum
    Donna Wilder, Fairfield Processing Corporation

Lynn Petrelli, Walmart Electronics and Film Department for assistance in keeping track of hundreds of slides of quilts.

Kelvin Kelso and the other staff members of the Camera Shop, Springfield, IL for picture-taking advice and assistance with equipment.

Rick Thompson, Frank Carlet and Dennis Penrod, Team Electronics, Springfield, IL for assistance in learning to use my new computer system and keeping it in operation.

Bill and Meredith Schroeder of The American Quilter's Society for their support and patience.

Sincere gratitude to a group of very special people whom I am privileged to call friends. None of them quilt, but all of them have given me support for my project the way that only friends who truly care can do:
    Junie and Richard Jenkinson, Schaumburg, IL
    Mary P. Kolb, Springfield, IL
    Chuck Lynch, Atlanta, GA
    Christine Nejmanowski, Carlinville, IL
    Carolyn Schwartz, Carlinville, IL
    Jacqueline K. Thomas, Carlinville, IL

Joe Barber, my husband. Chris and Steve, my sons.

Foreword

Even at our first meeting, Rita Barber's enthusiasm for quilting and her desire to help quilters was evident. It was at the Houston Quilt Festival -- that wonderful array of quilts from all over the country -- that I met Rita. Examining a quilt with intricate convex and concave curves flowing across it, I marveled at the quilter's skill and muttered, "I can't figure it out." Rita, standing beside me, overheard my remark and immediately began to explain the intricacies of the pieced construction. From that chance encounter, I met Rita the quilter, Rita the historian and Rita the researcher, who had a compelling desire to tell the stories of Illinois quilters.

Although she was aware of the merit of preserving these stories, she was not sure of the best strategy. Would it be an Illinois Quilt Project patterned after that superb example of the Kentucky Quilt Project? Would it be a permanent or traveling exhibit?

Listening to the many stories of quilters, she felt a book would give visibility to their quilts and voice to their stories -- their comments, their dreams, the poignancy of their daily lives. Her desire, it seemed, was to let the quilter speak to reveal her thoughts on quilting.

In her effort to give identity to otherwise unknown quilters, she interviewed countless Illinoisans. From these interviews she has selected story pieces as carefully as the quilter selects bits of cloth -- both quilter and author wanting to create a lasting remembrance.

Rita's meticulous care to quote accurately enables the reader to gain an intimacy with the quilters in the book. The simplicity and directness of Rita's technique -- to let the quilter speak with only limited commentary from the author -- has made this book a small treasure. The reader, like Rita's grandmother, will want to sit on the steps in the sunshine and there meet new friends as she reads the patchwork of stories in *Somewhere in Between*.

Virginia Ferrill Piland
Palatine, Illinois
1986

Preface

This book is the result of an interest in quilts, quilters and quilting that started in 1962 when I made three small quilts for the child I was expecting.

In 1982, another quilter, Madeline Hawley, asked if I would participate in a project similar to the much publicized Kentucky Quilt Project. The project evolved into this book.

This book is not meant to be an academic study although it is as well researched as time and money have permitted. It contains the stories and experiences associated with the quilts shown. These are for the most part women's stories. Quilts and/or stories were chosen which had a tie to Illinois, that could be documented and that had received little or no recent publicity.

Women often asked, "Why would you want to know about me or my quilts?" It often took encouragement, but finally the responses came. Now they will not remain a part of the silent multitude of the women of our past.

The Early Years

A militia bill in the South Carolina Department of Archives for articles lost during a skirmish of the Revolutionary War reads:

> "To Josiah Downen Being in the Servis of this State under Command of Genl. Pickens and sent out on a Detachment under the command of Col. Hays was overtaken by a part of the enemy and was run in flight the above Josiah Downen was struck off his horse and lay sometime as Dead at which time he Left one Riffel gun Sadel bridel one cover lid on Quilt a wen Raccoon Hat one Silver plated Spur".

A quilt is listed among the lost articles for which Josiah sought and received reimbursement. Quilts were a part of the lives of the people of the colonies as they are a part of the lives of many people today.

Quilts moved westward with families as they explored and settled this country.

Josiah Downen and his family were among those who moved westward from the Carolinas to Kentucky, Indiana and eventually to Illinois. In 1859, Josiah's grandson, Thomas, his six sons and all their family moved to Gallatin County, Illinois. Descendants of Josiah own much southern Illinois property around Ridgeway, New Haven and Shawneetown.

Today, seven generations later, his granddaughter, Kay Pyle Hudec is a quilter, making quilts in much the same way as the quilt that Josiah lost. Raised at Carmi near the Illinois-Indiana border, Kay remembers her mother quilting on frames that were handed down through the family. Kay now lives in Kingwood, Texas. She quilts with a group called the "Quilt Batts" and is involved with a state-wide quilt research project.

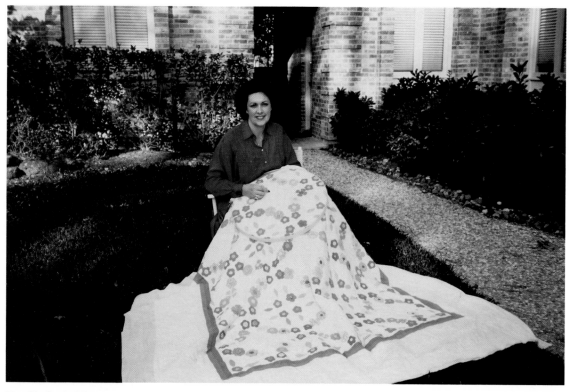

Kay Hudec holding the most recent group effort of the Quilt Batts, a quilt bee composed of seven women who have created and quilted together for six years. This quilt is an original design made for a very special quilter, Diane Klefstad, who has moved to New Orleans. Kay said, "The Quilt Batts are really special to me - they are inspiration and 'group therapy.' I understand the quilting bees of yesteryear by being a part of a continuing tradition."

Quilts are cherished in the Downen family. A look through the Downen Family Book, a geneology published in 1974 depicts family quilts, too. A picture of Leatha Downen Givens (1863-1932) and her husband, Bill, is taken with an OCEAN WAVE quilt as the backdrop. Quilts form a backdrop in several other family pictures included in the geneology.

Family members still refer to Leatha and Bill as "Pa and Ma Givens". For some unknown reason, they took their son Lawrence's oldest child, Marie to raise when another child was born. Marie's son, Bill Medlin and his wife, Zella, still have quilts from "Ma Givens". The quilt shown is a FLOWER BASKET with the basket pieced and the flowers appliqued over the basket with buttonhole stitches.

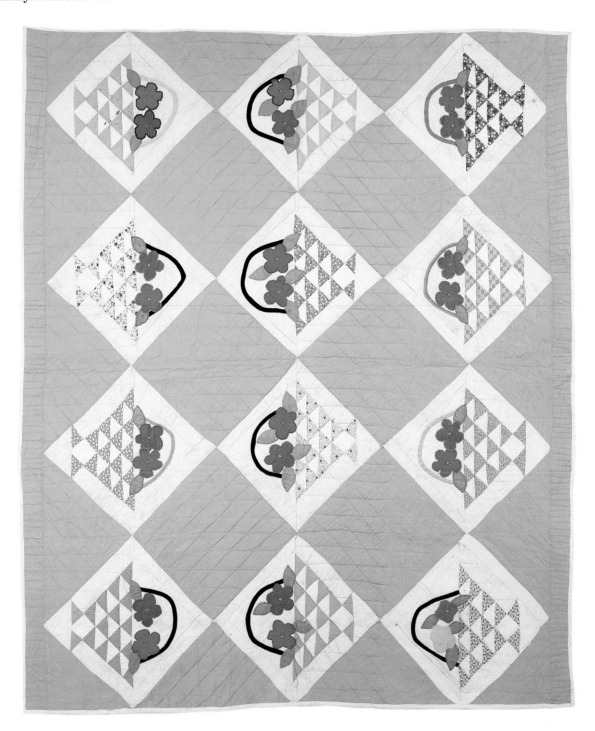

FLOWER BASKET, Circa 1920, 70″ x 84″. Attributed to Leatha Downen Givens. Owned by William and Zella Medlin.

The current generation of the Downen family includes an avid quilt collector. Ann Dague Swan collects quilts from her family (Downen) and from her husband's as well. "I don't quilt . . . yet," she says. She has received quilts from her mother's sister, Blanche Moye Cook as well as others in the family.

One of these quilts is an OCEAN WAVE, pieced and quilted by Oleva Downen Edwards, Ann's great-grandmother. Oleva made the quilt before her marriage and her mother, Rebecca Culley Downen, helped her quilt it.

OCEAN WAVE, Circa 1880, 65″ x 85″. Pieced by Oleva Downen Edwards and quilted by her and her mother, Rebecca Culley Downen. Owned by Ann Dague Swan.

Blanche and her husband, Don, live on a century farm. The farm has been in the family over one hundred years. She has quilts that were pieced by her grandmother and mother. When they take the quilts out to look at them and touch them, the names of family members and quilts run together in conversation--Mary Zerelda Carr's PERSIAN ROSE, Cora Edwards' FAN, Ruth Moye Dague's TUMBLER . . .

The PERSIAN ROSE quilt owned by Blanche was a joint project. The small flowers were pieced by Mary Zerelda Carr, Blanche's paternal grandmother. Cora Edwards Moye, Blanche's mother then finished the top and Blanche helped to quilt it. The quilt was made before 1946.

PERSIAN ROSE (also called BABY ASTER), Circa 1940, 72″ x 84″. Pieced by Mary Zeralda Carr and Cora Edwards Moye, quilted by them and Blanche Moye Cook. Owned by Blanche Moye Cook.

From another part of the family, Edith Hill Downen, 82, is still quilting. She has quilted since she was a child. She really doesn't remember when she learned. She has quilted all kinds of quilts, mostly from scraps. Patterns are made or swapped. "Joinings" or linings are bought; scraps are swapped too, in order to get more variety.

It's the quilting that she loves. She still goes to Omaha to quilt at the Senior Citizens Center where quilts are brought to be quilted. Fees begin at thirty-five dollars and Edith says the "older ones" in the quilting group at the center determine the fee for the quilting of a particular top.

One quilt of Edith's, a FAN, is a common pattern with a sad story. Edith's two daughters, Blanche Berneda, 11, and Ida Lou, 3, both died within a year. Edith's mother, Lucretia Moye Hill, pieced the quilt from the clothing of the two children. Together, she and Edith quilted it.

The quilt has a softness and mellowness about it, partly from age, partly from the arrangement of color. The base of the fan is brown. As she stood telling the story, with the quilt spread on a bed beneath a picture of the two little girls she said, "Well, there were all those clothes you see . . ." She did not really finish the sentence. She said no more of that quilt and went on to others in the stack.

The Downen girls.

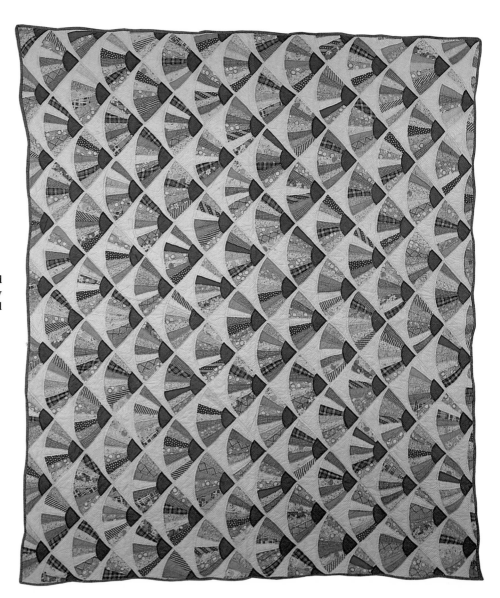

FAN, Circa 1938, 70″ x 82″. Pieced by Lucretia Moye Hill and quilted by her and Edith Hill Downen. Owned by Edith Hill Downen.

In still another part of the Downen family, Pearl Rister Ramsey, 88, has special quilts too. Quilts made by her maternal grandmother, Sarah Frances Price McGhee, who was born in 1840 and by her mother, Emily McGhee Rister. She remembers many "quiltings" as a child growing up - the fun, the sharing.

But the quilt in which she seemed to take the most pride is a new quilt made in 1981 for her and her husband, Jesse, on the occasion of their 65th wedding anniversary.

The quilt was the idea of her son, Charles, one of their five children. Each of the blocks in the quilt was made by one of the children or grandchildren and depicts something special to that particular person.

Charles' block is made with surgical suture thread. After all, he is a doctor.

By the time the Downen family had come to Illinois, it had been a state for 40 years and had grown in population and development. Although it was still a rural state with vast areas of untilled prairie, several cities had grown to considerable size with Chicago being the largest. The opening of the Erie Canal and the development of a network of roads and railroads had changed the previous pattern of settlement.

Earlier immigrants had come to the Illinois territory either by boat up the Mississippi or over land by horse or wagon. Population lay in the southern section along the Ohio, Wabash and Mississippi rivers that formed the borders of the state and provided its main connection with the outside world. What would become the bustling city of Chicago was a small settlement on the lake and between the two areas there was wilderness.

In reading the most commonly recommended histories of the exploration and settlement of Illinois, one finds few women mentioned. However, the Lakeside Classics, a series dealing with a variety of Americana contains two books written by women. This situation is addressed in remarks by historian and editor, Milo M. Quaife in his historical introduction to one of the books, *A Woman's Story of Pioneer Illinois*.

"The most famous son of Illinois is credited with a saying to the effect that God must love the common people, since he has made so many of them. Reasoning from similar grounds it may be asserted that God regards the female sex at least as highly as the male. But the reader of the pages of recorded history would never be led to suspect this. Why, it is not my present purpose to inquire; rather, having called attention to the fact, I wish to show the significance of Mrs. Tillson's narrative. Commonly, history is written by men and from the masculine point of view. The interests, the labors, the ideals and achievements of the gentler half of society are taken for granted or left to the imagination. The inadequacy, not to say the injustice, of such a portrayal of history is self-evident. With unerring finger and with pen more magic than my own the latest historian of the cow country, America's last frontier, has pointed to the woman in the sunbonnet as the supreme figure in the history of the West:

"The chief figure of the American West, the figure of the age, is not the long-haired, fringed-legginged man riding a raw-boned pony, but the gaunt and sad-faced woman sitting on the front seat of the wagon, following her lord where he might lead, her face hidden in the same ragged sunbonnet which had crossed the Appalachians and the Missouri long before. That was America, my brethern! There was the seed of America's wealth the woman in the sunbonnet; and not, after all the hero with the rifle across his saddle horn. Who has written her story? Who has painted her picture?"

Christiana Homes Tillson and Rebecca Burlend did write their stories and their words will be mentioned here. Others, who could, kept journals and diaries and many of those are being researched and published. Those who could not write left us another history of things they made, including quilts. Most of the things were necessary to daily living, but they were made so that they added beauty to the commonly sparse and meager lives of early settlers.

Rebecca Burlend was from Yorkshire, England. In her narrative, *A True Picture of Emmigration*, she says, "I gave up the idea of ending my days in my own country with the utmost reluctance, and should never have become an emigrant, if obedience to my husband's wishes had left me any alternative." John Burlend, a tenant farmer barely making an existance for his family, decided to see what could be done in the western world.

The family with five children came to the United States on the vessel "Home" in 1831. Their two eldest, a son and daughter were left behind. While on the ship and upon leaving sight of England she thought . . . "there were many on board, who, as well as myself, felt a gratification in gazing at the naked rocks that projected from the land that had given us birth; . . . til quite weary with looking I descended into the cabin, and endeavoured to be reconciled to my situation by exercising myself in some necessary employment."

The tiresome days at sea gave her time to think . . . "Yes, many a time when mirth and noise have been the prevailing order on deck, have I sought retirement to muse upon the past, and pry into the future. I own such conduct was unwise; I should have been happier if I could have mingled in the diversions of my companions: but reader, knowest thou not when the heart is sick the very means which would be beneficial are often the most repulsive?"

The ship landed in New Orleans and the family took a riverboat north on the Mississippi to be left on the riverbank in the dark . . . "standing by the brink of the river, bordered by a dark wood, with no one near to notice us or tell us where we might procure accommodation or find harbour . . . the evening shades were rapidly settling on the earth . . . above me was the chill blue canopy of heaven, a wide river before me and a dark wood behind."

A fearful landing in a new land after a long trip at sea and a reluctant beginning to the journey. Hardship had only just begun. Even getting candles helped because "Hitherto the light of the fire had served us instead of a candle, which was very inconvenient, as I wished to sew a little in the evenings." Inadequate lighting was only a portion of the problem, fabric was not plentiful and "for a yard of common printed calico, they asked half a dollar, or a bushel of wheat . . ."

How often do we follow Rebecca's actions and thoughts today—losing ourselves and our problems in some "necessary employment," knowing we should be busy but not having the motivation and worrying about the cost of goods?

In 1846, Rebecca returned to England to visit her son and daughter. When she returned to Illinois the daughter, Mary and her husband, Luke Yelliot, came with her. The quilts shown were made by Hanna Croft Yelliot, wife of Mary's son John. The owners are descendants of the Burlends.

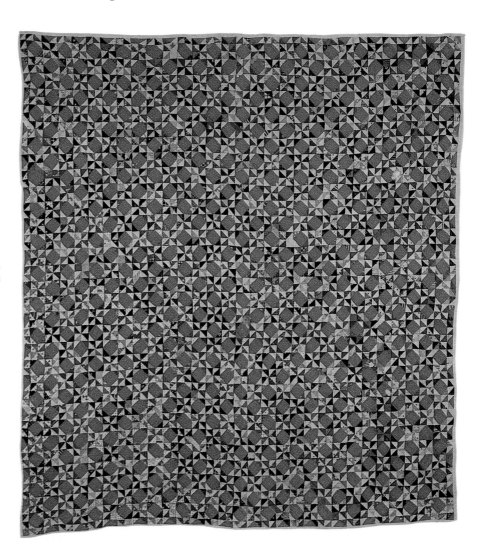

WINDMILL, Circa 1920, 64″ x 78″. Pieced and quilted by Hanna Croft Yelliot. Owned by John Sheppard.

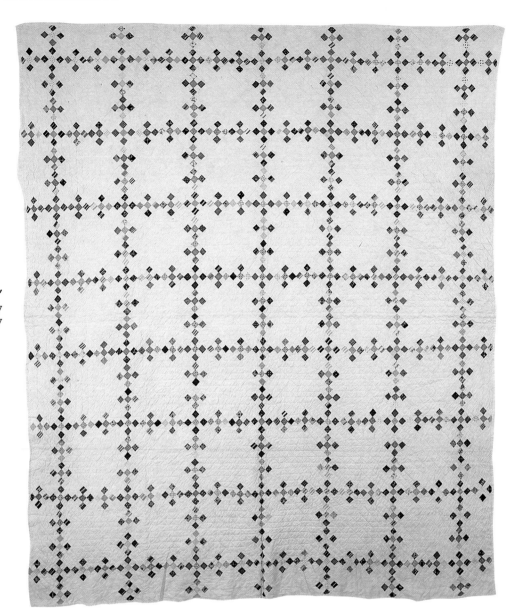

IRISH CHAIN, Circa 1920, 64″ x 84″. Pieced and quilted by Hanna Croft Yelliot. Owned by Catherine Sheppard Moore.

Another of the Lakeside Classics is *A Woman's Story of Pioneer Illinois*. Christiana Holmes Tillson of Massachusetts married in October of 1822. Her bridal trip was the overland trek to Illinois where her husband had been living since 1819. In describing a night's lodging on that trip she said, ''There was but one room in the main cabin, which I at once perceived was unusually clean for an establishment of that kind. There were two beds nicely made, with clean pillows and handsome bed-quilts, the floor clean and the coarse chairs looking as if they had just been scrubbed.''

The belongings which they had shipped were long in arriving and they were in their own lodgings before receiving them. She noted . . . ''Hired a bed and quilt from Mr. Rountree, with whom we had expected to board.'' With winter coming on, the delay of the shipment became a very real problem so,

''As we were not abundantly supplied, I undertook the making of a comfortable

. . . but where, O where, was the cotton to be found! I knew everybody had their ''cotton patches'' and raised their own cotton, but in trying to buy, found that they only picked it from seed in small quantities. While I was puzzling myself what to do, Mr. Wright brought from his farm some twelve pounds of cotton in the seed; when separated two-thirds would be seed and the remaining third cotton. I then commenced the arduous task of separating the cottom from the seed, and after much labor and wear and tear of fingers I succeeded in getting enough to fill a comfortable. It had to be carded and made into bats before it could be used, and fortunately my maid-of-all-work knew how to card. But the cards: where were they to be found? After much inquiry I heard of some one who was willing to lend her ''kairds'' to a Yankee woman. So the cotton was carded, after about a week's labor by Joicy, and meanwhile Loomis had made a quilting frame and the great affair of making a comfortable was accomplished.''

Christiana's lot was far better than that of most frontier women. She was educated and assisted her husband at his work with her writing skills. Because they had more wealth than most she had some advantages in the wholly frontier society in which they lived. When writing her narrative for her youngest daughter who had been born too late to know of the ''good old days of the frontier'', she said,

''the accumulation of comforts, and the luxuries and improvements forty or fifty years have brought, and which are here so liberally enjoyed, forbid the realization of frontier life to those who have not by stern experience passed through such an ordeal; and though we may have many pleasant recollections, I think, as a whole, the retrospect is preferable to the reality. Few would like to again pass through the bitterness for the sake of enjoying the remembrance of the few sweets.''

The immigration of George Vennum and his family from Ohio in 1834 was delayed by the birth of daughter, Mary Ann. A quilt made by Mary Ann Vennum is now in the collection of the Iroquois County Historical Society Museum. Although the quilt is signed, it is not dated. The use of the name Vennum would indicate that it was done before her first marriage in 1852.

FEATHERED STAR (with trapunto), Circa 1850. 75″ x 82″. Pieced and quilted by Mary Ann Vennum. Owned by the Iroquois County Historical Society Museum, Watseka.

From today's point of view, when many women never achieve fine needlework skills, it is difficult to look at the fine workmanship in Mary Ann's quilt and understand that it was probably made by a young woman of 18 or younger. The quilt is a FEATHERED STAR of indigo blue with white squares joining the stars. The solid white squares are embellished with stuffed work in several designs and the border with its tiny sawtooth trim features a stuffed work vine.

The patience and detail of her quilting were reflected in her life. She survived two husbands and had eight children. In her obituary published in the Watseka Republican on August 11, 1915, she is described as follows:

"Her life was a busy one and her domestic duties were sometimes arduous, but she always found time to perform her numerous church duties . . . She was a charter member of the Methodist Church and was the leading spirit of its Sunday School. She and her husband were also prominent in the temperance work of the day and whatever was for the betterment of the community found in her a champion."

Just prior to the Civil War, Martha Parks Austin Stanley (1821-1908) and her family moved from Missouri to a farm near Alton, Illinois. Family stories say she did not want to be part of a slave state. Her second husband, Norman Stanley, was the business partner of her first husband, William Hoy. They were merchants who sold wheat fans, a type of farm machinery. Martha had returned with her child to her home in Ohio after the deaths of her first husband and another child. Norman went to Ohio and brought her back to live in Missouri and then Illinois.

ROCKY ROAD TO KANSAS, Circa 1860, 64″ x 64″. Pieced and quilted by Martha Parks Austin Stanley. Owned by Jean Landon Ashworth.

Their daughter, Joie Stanley Hoblit, was an artist and wife of A. Lincoln Hoblit founder of the Carlinville National Bank. The bank is still an important part of the community (Carlinville, Illinois) and family members are still involved in its operation. Joie painted the portrait of her mother, Martha.

Martha spent her later years in the home of one of her children. Her time was spent doing needlework of various kinds including quilting. Her work includes several silk and velvet quilts which are still in the family. The quilts shown belong to Jean Landon Ashworth and the portrait to Joie Landon Russell of Carlinville, both of whom are great-granddaughters of Martha.

Portrait of Martha Parks Austin Stanley by her daughter, Josie Stanley Hoblit. Owned by Joie Landon Russell.

PINEAPPLE, unfinished (also called WINDMILL BLADES, Log Cabin Variation), Circa 1860, 62″ x 72″. Pieced by Martha Parks Austin Stanley. Owned by Jean Landon Ashworth.

Another quilt from the mid-1800's belongs to Pauline Hills of Modesto. The quilt was purchased in 1938 somewhere in the eastern part of the country by Bessie Woodruff Wendnagle (Mrs. Eugene) of Chicago. It was given to Pauline in 1959 as a gift of appreciation.

Although initialed in the lower right-hand corner the quilt is not dated. The monogram, "B.J.", is ap-

UNNAMED, Circa mid-1800s, 72″ x 84″. Owned by Pauline Hills. Photographs by Rita B. Barber.

plied to the quilt with pieced letters. Lettering of this type is the topic of an article by Winifred Reddall appearing in *Uncoverings*, 1980, a publication of the American Quilt Study Group. A search of available literature produced seven quilts with pieced lettering of the type on the Hills' quilt. The quilts dated from 1833 to 1891. Of the quilts, four were from upstate New York, one from New Jersey and another from Connecticut. The seventh is described as "probable New England origin." Dated 1848 and made by Maria Cadman Hubbard, it is shown in the *Treasury of American Quilts* by Cyril I. Nelson and Carter Houck.

An even earlier quilt with this type of lettering is pictured in *The Knopf Collectors' Guides to American Antiques: Quilts, Coverlets, Rugs & Samplers* by Robert Bishop. The center section contains the pieced intials "HDB", the date "1807" and several small design motifs.

The Hills' quilt is of navy and white dotted cotton fabric appliqued on a white ground. The large "potted tree" motifs resemble a cut-paper design and form a negative heart shape in the center. Smaller motifs include clusters of oak leaves which also contain negative hearts at the center of each leaf. Birds, stars and a vine of grapes and grape leaves form the

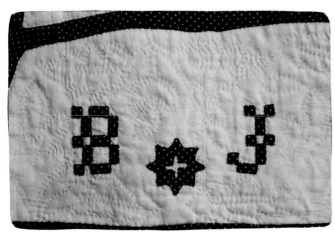

Close up of applied initials.

border. Because of the hearts in the design it has been said the quilt may have been a betrothal or wedding quilt. There are design similarities in the motifs of this piece and the work of Pennsylvania German settlers as well. Although their work often shows this "cut-paper" type of design, bold colors are commonly used. Blue and white is seen only occasionally. In addition, hearts are common motifs in Pennsylvania German designs. In this context they are not necessarily used to denote a betrothal.

Many quilts from the earlier periods of Illinois history have become part of museum collections. Three quilts from the mid-1800's form part of the Illinois State Museum collection. Information from the museum files gives us some background on the items. A lovely example of trapunto (stuffed work) is a baby quilt, designed by John Robert Degge and quilted by his wife, Mary Frances Degge of Petersburg for their daughter, Mary Frances. The urn in the center features tulips and daisies and is bordered by a swagged floral vine with pineapple motifs in the corners. The quilt was donated to the museum by Catherine Degge Mars, a younger daughter of the Degges.

The floral applique quilt with its stylized flowers and berries is circa 1860, made by Elizabeth Sutherland Jones (1793-1877) of Decatur. The applique is done in red, green and orange cotton on a white cotton ground. The binding is green and the hand quilting is in diagonal rows across the quilt. It is inscribed "Leonard Ashton/Morris/Grundy Co./Ills" in ink on the back. Leonard Ashton was Mrs. Jones' son-in-law. He ran a store in Morris where his shipments of merchandise came wrapped in pieces of material which he saved for his mother-in-law to use in quiltmaking. The quilt was donated to the museum by Mrs. Harry G. Woodruff of Decatur, a great-granddaughter of the maker.

The third quilt from this collection is a lively applique with patriotic and religious motifs. It was made by Helen Minerva Gilchrist (1831-1912) who came with her family to Hills Grove, McDonough County, Illinois, in 1834.

When she was twelve, she was sent to live with an aunt in New York where she attended a school for young ladies. The quilt may have been made between 1847 and 1848 since it has 20 stars placed over the central eagle. Twenty-nine states had been admitted to the union by that time. The embroidery in the upper right motif reads: "HOLY BIBLE/THE/LIGHT/ OF THE WORLD AND/THE GUIDE OF OUR/ NATION".

These stories and quilts represent those who came to Illinois from the time it was a territory through its becoming a state and surviving a civil war. Many events which now are synonomous with Illinois had occurred during this period. Chicago had been settled, grown, burned and rebuilt. Abraham Lincoln, a lawyer, had been elected president, led the nation through Civil War and been assassinated. The stockyards grew with the railroads and farmers grew more corn and wheat than any other state. Outside the major cities, rural life was still difficult even though times were prosperous. By the last years of the nineteenth century, Illinois was the third largest state behind New York and Pennsylvania and Chicago, the nation's second largest city. With industrialization and unionization, Illinois entered the twentieth century.

TRAPUNTO CRADLE, Circa 1850, 46″ x 40″. Designed by John Robert Degge and made by Mary Francis Degge. From the collection of the Illinois State Museum. Photograph by Marlin Roos.

UNNAMED APPLIQUE, Circa 1860, 69″ x 92″. Made by Elizabeth Sutherland Jones. From the collection of the Illinois State Museum. Photograph by Marlin Roos.

UNNAMED APPLIQUE, Circa 1840-1850, 92″ x 92″. Made by Helen Minerva Gilchrist. From the collection of the Illinois State Museum. Photograph by Marlin Roos.

At the beginning of the new century Illinois was in the national spotlight. In 1906, a federal meat inspection act was passed largely because of publicity surrounding the publication of a novel, *The Jungle*, by Sinclair Lewis. The novel dealt with the Chicago stockyards and drew much attention to Chicago and the meat industry.

Prohibition, women's suffrage, political scandal and reform, the Mafia and union strikes kept Illinois prominent in national news. In spite of negative publicity, Illinois was prospering. A superb system of railroads provided transportation for travelers and freight shippers. The highway system was developed after the first quarter of the century. The mail traveled by air as early as 1912 and aviation business began to develop in the state. Rural electrification started to bring some of the benefits of modern technology to the farming areas of the state.

The celebration of the Illinois Centennial coincided with the involvement of America in global war, World War I. The people of Illinois joined with the rest of the country in leading to an Allied victory. During the 1920's, most of the residents of the state prospered but the prosperity was stopped by the Great Depression for Illinoisians as it was for most of the country.

The Depression Years

The Great Depression of 1929 brought a revival in quiltmaking from the decline it had seen at the end of the nineteenth century. General prosperity, mail order businesses and the general availability of inexpensive blankets and bedcovers along with other manufactured goods were partly responsible for the decline. But during the decade of the Thirties, women were encouraged to do all the forms of needlework. Newspapers and women's magazines had advertisements, articles, patterns, kits and contests related to needlework.

An Illinois resident of this period who participated in many of the contests was Bertha Sheram (Sheramsky) Stenge (Mrs. Bernard, 1891-1957). Her quilts are a combination of originality, creativity and superb craftsmanship based on traditional patterns, quilting traditions and contemporary themes. She is counted among the outstanding quiltmakers of the first half of this century.

Mrs. Stenge's quilts in the collections of the Art Institute of Chicago and the Chicago Historical Society are shown. The remainder are in private collections. The TOBY LIL quilt was named for the Toby jugs featured in some of the fabrics used and to honor Lillian Fuchsmann who was a friend of Mrs. Stenge. Some of the fabrics in the quilt date from the 19th century. The CHICAGO FAIR quilt features Chicago-related images including a Chicago Fire scene in the quilting. It was exhibited and won Honorable Mention at the Century of Progress Exposition, Chicago, 1933.

Quilts by Mrs. Stenge received a great deal of publicity through fairs, exhibits, magazine and newspaper articles. Among the exhibits where her quilts won numerous ribbons and prizes were Cook County Fair (Illinois), Illinois State Fair, Kentucky State Fair, 1933 Century of Progress Chicago Exposition, Eastern States Exposition in Massachusetts, 1940 New York World's Fair (Grand Prize), the 1936 Canadian National Exhibition and the 1950 Women's International Exposition in New York. The quilts were also featured in a one-day exhibition at the Smithsonian Institute and in one-woman shows at the University of California Art Gallery and the Art Institute of Chicago.

Some of the magazines featuring her work were the *Ladies Home Journal, Woman's Day* (Grand Prize in National Needlework Contest, 1942) and the *Stearns and Foster Company's Mountain Mist Blue Book of Prize Quilts-State Fair Prize Winners* (1950).

Mrs. Stenge was generous with her time and her quilts. Her correspondence with hundreds of people indicates that she took the time to answer their inquiries for information, patterns, informal "quilt shows" in her home and as she traveled about the country. She took the time to carefully file her correspondence which included the great names of quilting in that period – Carrie Hall, Marie Webster, Florence Peto and Elizabeth Wells Robertson.

Twenty-five quilts are mentioned by name in various articles about Mrs. Stenge and there are others. The number of quilts in itself is an accomplishment most quilters would be proud to claim. But an examination of her work "in the cloth" leaves the beholder in awe of the skill of technique and design which rightfully earned Mrs. Stenge her reputation as a master quilter of America.

TOBY LIL, 1951. Made by Bertha Sheram Stenge. From the collection of the Art Institute of Chicago.

CHICAGO FAIR, 1933. Made by Bertha Sheram Stenge. From the collection of the Chicago Historical Society.

The Middle Years

Although needlework of all types was created during the middle decades of this century, quilting was not as common in many areas as it had been. Needlework patterns and kits were still published and women's magazines still had needlework sections. Strong cultural movements were taking place in the country that would be the foundation of a strong new involvement with quilts. The feminist movement with its resulting recognition of the importance of women's history was a contributing factor. Quilting was for the most part, women's work. When studied, that work tells much about the women and the culture in which they produced it.

The 1971 exhibit of quilts held at the Whitney Museum of American Art is frequently cited as a focal point in the consolidation of quilt enthusiasts into the vigorous group they have become. The exhibit focused on the aesthetics of quilts as a design form. The quilts were from the collection of Johnathan Holstein and Gail van der Hoof of New York. The exhibit was not without precedent. In 1963 the Denver Art Museum Quilt Collection catalog was published. The Newark Museum held the "Optical Quilts" exhibit in 1965 and the Art Institute of Chicago, held the "American Quilts" exhibit in 1966.

These exhibits, others that followed and a book by Jonathan Holstein, *The Pieced Quilt: An American Design Tradition* published in 1972, helped solidify the revived interest in quilting. Until the publication of this book, most of the literature available had been published prior to 1950. One notable exception was Dolores Hinson's *Quilting Manual*, in 1966. Holstein's book was followed in 1974 by the book *Quilts in America* by Myron and Patsy Orlofsky. Both books continue to be key resources for persons with an interest in quilting. A current list of books for quilters numbers in the hundreds. Another occurence which gave great support to the quilter was the publication of several magazines just for quilters.

These events and the Bicentennial celebration events which were held all over the country during the mid-1970s gave support to the study of our past. Quilting was a strong part of that study. Quilt shows became an integral part of events held to celebrate our heritage with designs, kits and competitions for Bicentennial quilts flourishing.

One such event, a part of Illinois Celebration '76, was the exhibit and catalog of "200 Years of American Quilts in Illinois Private Collections." The catalog describes the exhibit as a comprehensive view of the quiltmaker's art in Illinois. It was part of a traveling exhibition program entitled "Two Hundred Years of Illinois Art."

At the Clayville Rural Life Center just west of Springfield, quilts are exhibited and quilting demonstrated. This restored historical site has included quilting for many years and as locals there will be quick to tell you, "You have to meet Fleta Grieme."

Around Springfield, Fleta Carter Grieme personifies traditional quilting. She has quilted for herself and others for more years than she sometimes cares to remember. Now in her eighties, in a long calico dress and mobcap and seated at a frame, she reminisced about the first quilt show at Clayville. "Awhile back Doris and I went to a big show in Lincoln, Nebraska and it made me feel like about that tall . . . They are going about it in such a big way . . . We took a rope and hung it from one door of the barn to the other, and it had quilts on it and people came and we had a good time." Today the quilt show fills several rooms, the rails of the balcony and spills over into the yard, still on ropes. People still come. And they still have a good time.

Fleta learned to quilt from her grandmother, Mary Bell Strobe, and her mother, Edna Strobe Carter. To her and other women of her generation quilts were meant to be used. She had five quilts at her marriage and they got used up. Just a fragment of one of them was left so she turned it under and hemmed it on the sewing machines so it could be used when one of many visiting babies came. But her granddaughter saw it and wanted to save it. "Imagine that!," she said, "we always used quilts, not saved them." When asked how many she supposed she had made, she replied, "Oh, I lost count long ago."

The TRIP AROUND THE WORLD quilt that remains one of her favorites was made by her mother. Fleta enjoys telling the story of that quilt.

"She must have started it about 1918 but with all us kids there wasn't much time for her to quilt. She worked on it a long time. Finally, one day she said, 'I'm going to die someday so I'd better get to it and finish that quilt'."

It was finished about 1945. Fleta likes to point out the variety of fabrics from the different times. She also says her mother chose a very smart way to quilt such tiny pieces (just over one half inch square). She turned the quilt to the back, marked an all-over fan design and then quilted from the back. This permitted her to avoid many of the hundreds of seams and achieve more even quilting.

The pieced TURKEY TRACKS quilt was made for grandson, Mark Estrop. She picked the pattern because her grandson is director for church camping activities and had acquired the nickname, "Turkey Man."

Fleta and her friends – Helen Parsons, Marianna Sausaman, and Marge Kessel – have met and quilted together for "about 30 years". Quilting never died for them. She belongs to the recently formed Q.U.I.L.T.S. Guild in Springfield. Fleta has been involved with the repair of some of the items in the collection of the Lincoln Home. She has judged many quilt shows including the prestigious Illinois State Fair show. To Fleta "the best part of the quilt is the quilting" and good quilting is "a matter of being meticulous."

TRIP AROUND THE WORLD, 1945, 74″ x 84″. Made by Edna Strobe Carter. Shown with owner, Fleta Carter Grieme.

TURKEY TRACKS, 1982, 82″ x 96″. Made by Fleta Carter Grieme. Owned by Mark Estrop.

Recent Years

Doris Waltman Krake was instrumental in founding the Q.U.I.L.T.S. Guild and served as its first president. Q.U.I.L.T.S. stands for "quilters united in learning, teaching and self-improvement." She teaches in an elementary school and one of her projects for the children is a quilted pillow top. She also teaches quilting in community classes and area quilting events, gives demonstrations at Clayville and Rockome Gardens.

Her repetition of hints and ideas during demonstrations led to the printing of step-by-step directions for over ninety quilt patterns. Most of the patterns are traditional ones but several are of her own design including ILLINOIS CROSSROADS, DOGWOOD, and SUGAR & SPICE which was inspired by the traditional DRUNKARD'S PATH pattern. In addition, she published a book, *Sampler Quilt Primer*.

Another avid Springfield quilter is Marian Brockschmidt. More involved with softball and basketball as a child, Marian learned to embroidery when she was about seven. At the age of twelve, Marian did the embroidery on a butterfly quilt that her mother made. Her mother made all the clothes for Marian and her two sisters and made numerous quilts. Her quilts got hard use and none remain.

Marian began entering competitions in 1975. She jokingly credits sibling rivalry with really getting her moving with her quilting. A niece had encouraged her sister, Ruth Neitzel of Merriville, Indiana, to enter a quilt in the 1974 National Quilting Association competition where it won a blue ribbon and the Viewer's Choice ribbon. Marion got busy and finished her STATE BIRDS AND FLOWERS quilt. It was entered in the 1975 Illinois State Fair where it won first place and best quilt awards, as well as best embroidery and hand stitching awards. When she sent the quilt to the National Quilting Association competition, it won a blue ribbon, a special recognition ribbon and Viewer's Choice. It is shown in *Quilter's Newsletter* magazine, July 1976. "Such a thrill!" she said.

She has been a winner at the Illinois State Fair many years since 1975. Since she is a friend of Fleta Grieme, who judges that event, she says she never tells Fleta what her current project is. She has done several quilts which feature embroidery. Her STATE BIRDS AND FLOWERS, BLOSSOM TIME and ABC quilts all exhibit detailed research in design and meticulous technique in construction.

Another such quilt is the Bicentennial quilt which she named GREAT AMERICANS. It features great Americans with Indians representing the beginning of the country and astronauts representing the present. A detail of the Lincoln section is shown. The quilt received "only a second" at the National Quilting Association Show and is shown in the May 1977 issue of *Patchwork Patter*, the magazine of the National Quilting Association. It also won a first place in the *Quilter's Newsletter* Bicentennial quilt competition and is featured on the front cover of the December 1976 issue of that magazine.

Abraham Lincoln Block from Marian Brockschmidt's GREAT AMERICANS quilt.

GREAT AMERICANS, 1976, 96″ x 102″. Made and owned by Marian Brockschmidt.

Her most recent achievement will be hard to beat. In addition to being a state fair winner, her GRANDMOTHER'S ENGAGEMENT RING won the Mountain Mist 1985 Quilt Contest sponsored by the Stearns Technical Textile Company. She received a purchase prize of $1,250 and a Caribbean cruise. The award was announced during an awards presentation and reception at Quilt Festival in Houston, Texas. One hundred finalists' quilts were exhibited. Marian could not attend and was called with information of her winning. She later said, "It seemed so long between the phone call and receiving any written confirmation of the award that I thought perhaps the call had been a dream."

Marian finds the time to be a member of the Q.U.I.L.T.S. Guild, collect dolls and make doll clothing (but not her own). She gives her husband credit for lots of tolerance and pride in her work. His only complaint has been a loose pin in the toe.

The Q.U.I.L.T.S. Guild of Springfield has many active members. Another of those members is Patricia Hoatson Abbott. In 1984, Pat's husband, Bud, decided it wasn't cold enough to make a trip to Florida and Pat decided to find something new to do. She had had a quilt made for a new grandchild and when she picked the quilt up, she wondered why she hadn't made it herself. She chose to take a class in quilting that was advertised at a Springfield quilt shop. While quilting was new and exciting to her, needlework was not. She quickly found the class projects too simple to be challenging.

She decided to make a FEATHERED STAR

GRANDMOTHER'S ENGAGEMENT RING, 1985. Made by Marian Brockschmidt. Owned by Stearns Technical Textiles Company (Mountain Mist Contest Winner, 1985.)

block. She says, "I laid the block out on the bed and decided it would make a great center for a quilt - and it grew "like Topsy". Pat took the quilt to Florida with her the following winter. She entered the un-quilted top in a Naples quilt show where it won Viewer's Choice. TOPSY, the finished quilt, measures 108″ x 120″. Pat entered the quilt in the juried American Quilter's Society Show in Paducah, Kentucky. TOPSY won third place for amateur patchwork and first place for the "First Quilt" category. The quilt is shown in the Fall 1985 issue of *American Quilter* magazine of the American Quilter's Society.

TOPSY, 1985, 108″ x 120″. Made and owned by Patricia Abbott.

Besides learning quilting at the class at A-1 Sewing, Pat made new friends. One of those friends is Carlene Gonzales Klickner. Carlene is also a member of Q.U.I.L.T.S. and the Decatur Quilters Guild as well. Recently chosen president of Q.U.I.L.T.S., she has been quilting five years. She makes quilts for home and family as well as quilted garments. Carlene calls herself a "very traditional quilter", meaning she uses traditional patterns and fabric combinations.

The friendship is now a business partnership as well. Pat and Carlene recently bought A-1 Sewing Center, the place where they met. The shop is now known as A-1/Quilters 2. They offer nearly 1,500 bolts of fabric plus patterns, books and notions all geared especially to the quilter. Classes are offered, too.

Classes like the one in which Pat and Carlene met are part of the ever increasing interest in quilting.

Although women have always helped each other learn to quilt and gathered together to quilt, the learning today differs from the learning experience of the past. Classes are held in fabric shops, in community education programs and as a part of general craft events. More significantly, events are being held around the country and in other parts of the world that are specifically about quilts and quilting. Conferences, symposiums, congresses, retreats – they are called by many names. They differ from shows and exhibits because they focus on gaining knowledge and skills, not just viewing a finished product.

These events are a part of a communication network for quilters that also features a range of publications, businesses and products. Guilds like Q.U.I.L.T.S. and the Decatur Quilters Guild educate their members and the public about quilting.

The Decatur Quilters Guild was founded in May, 1979, by six people who responded to an ad placed in a Decatur needlework shop by Madeline Kocher Hawley.

The first meetings were held monthly in the homes of members. By 1981, the guild had grown so much that the group could no longer be accommodated in private homes. The meetings were moved to the Lincoln Room of First Federal Savings & Loan where they are now held twice monthly.

In 1980, they held their first quilt show at Hickory Point Mall. After two shows held at Westminster Church, the show was moved to the Decatur Civic Center. Their sixth annual show in 1985 featured 175 quilts, wall-hangings and quilted garments as well as demonstrations, classes and merchants.

In 1983, the group became Chapter 187 of the National Quilting Association. It will host the 1986 National Quilting Association Show in Decatur. The group multiplied from six to 102 devoted members.

Madeline, founder and past president of the group, is an avid quilter, designer, researcher and teacher. She has National Quilting Association certification in both teaching and judging. Her wallhanging PUTTIN' ON THE RITZ is shown. She said the piece was inspired by an ad for the treatment of alcholism but didn't really look like the ad at all by the time she got it finished. It has been exhibited in several shows including the 1985 Decatur show.

PUTTIN' ON THE RITZ, 1985, 23" x 45".
Made and owned by Madeline Hawley.

Betty Marshall McMillion is another member of the Decatur Guild. Betty has been quilting for twenty-seven years. She learned to quilt from the members of the Ladies Aid at the Highlawn Church of God in St. Albans, West Virginia. Betty went to St. Albans as the seventeen-year-old bride of the minister. The ladies told her she had to help them earn money for the church or the pastor might not be paid. At the first quilting session she attended, she was given the tasks of keeping needles threaded and doing dishes at lunch time. After several sessions of doing dishes she asked why the other quilters didn't do dishes too. The answer was that good quilters were too valuable to spend time doing dishes. Betty promptly learned to quilt.

Her husband later went to a church in Salina, Ohio, where the ladies were dubious of her quilting skills. She was only twenty-eight years old. She wasn't long showing them she wouldn't be doing dishes at their quilting sessions.

Betty enjoys making quilts for her family. She has quilted for others, judged shows and written articles for publication in *Quilt World* magazine. Her quilt, GIANT DAHLIA has been shown in that magazine along with her original design, STAR IN THE WINDOW. Her wallhanging, GRANDMA'S HOUSE, has been featured on the cover.

Betty Marshall McMillion shown with some of her quilts including GIANT DAHLIA.

GRANDMA'S HOUSE belongs to her sister, Ruby Marshall Smith who will get the piece "someday". It has been busy being shown in various exhibits. The piece is Betty's interpretation of the country home of their grandmother, Ruby Ritchey Marshall. It depicts the hills of West Virginia with all the things she remembered about Grandma's house such as the poison ivy on the tree, the hunting dog and the swing on the porch.

GRANDMA'S HOUSE, 1984, 32″ x 44″. Made by Betty Marshall McMillion. Owned by Ruby Marshall Smith.

Her ENDLESS RIBBON quilt which is shown on the cover of this book is a pattern from Audrey Butterfield of the Quilting Barn in Rye, New Hampshire. The quilt was photographed at Fairview Park in Decatur. The log building is the old Macon County Courthouse. Records indicate that the young lawyer, Abraham Lincoln, attended the May 1838 term of the Macon County Circuit Court in the building and handled at least one case there. The courthouse has been restored and moved from the square to the park. Betty's husband, Collett, made the photos along with many others of her work. He enjoys traveling to quilt shows with her.

The Decatur Quilters Guild is one of more than twenty-five guilds in the state of Illinois. Not all quilters belong to organized guilds. Some quilters belong to church groups which provide quilting services to their communities and use any proceeds for the benefit of the church. Some groups of this type have been in existance for more than sixty years. Other quilters have "unofficial" groups or quilt solely on an individual basis.

Averil Mathis of Eldorado is one of those who does not belong to an established guild or group. She is known to many in the area as the "Quilt Lady." She is involved in many aspects of quilting including design, construction, collecting and study. As she has learned about quilts and quilting, she has moved from traditional to original design in her own work. Her INTERLOCKING ARROWS is an original design.

INTERLOCKING ARROWS, 1978, 56" x 71". Made and owned by Averil Mathis.

When she became involved in quilting, she gathered pictures and stories which she shared with many groups. One of her favorite quilt stories was told to her by a woman in her eighties. She calls it the "Egg Story." When she was young, the woman was part of a large family and they were each limited to one egg a day for breakfast. The young woman chose to eat an egg only one day a week and had her mother sell the other six for her. She used the money to buy fabric for her quilting.

In addition to quilts, Averil collects thimbles, sewing notions and sewing machines. She has written a book about thimbles, *Antique & Collectible Thimbles and Accessories*. Her husband, Noal, is a collector of stamps, clocks and Aladdin lamps. Some of Averil's projects combine their interests. The ALADDIN LAMP quilt shows several of the lamps in their collection. Noal won a similar quilt that was a joint project of Averil and several other women in the Aladdin Lamp Association.

ALADDIN LAMP, 1985, 80″ x 102″. Made by Averil Mathis. Owned by Noal Mathis.

Averill quilts "because it's something the ordinary person can do without having to be an accomplished artist." She keeps quilting because of the feeling of satisfaction when she has finished a project.

Although she does not belong to an established guild, Averil is part of a quilting group of sorts. Her friend, Ruth Reeder Brill, got her involved in quilting in 1973. Their friendship goes back to 1935 when Averil met Ruth at the church where Averil's father was pastor. Averil became an "adopted" sister to Ruth and her sisters, Ruby Reeder Murray and Hazel Reeder King. Their mother, Nora Mills Reeder, was known as "Mother Reeder" to family and friends. They all quilted.

Although Ruth, Hazel and Ruby had all learned to sew and had been somewhat involved with quilting as young women, they did not do a lot of it until 1966. They were looking for something their mother could do and quilting became a family project. The sisters would cut the pieces; their mother would do the piecing. Sometimes the sisters would set the top together. After the top was finished, Nora would do the quilting. She quilted for other people as well. They made many, many quilts, mostly of scraps. Nora quilted until her death at age 99.

Quilts shown from the Reeder family are FAN, RAIL FENCE, NOSEGAY and KALEIDOSCOPE. Ruth said she, Averil and Noal made the KALEIDOSCOPE from a Kodak picture. Averil said the GIANT DAHLIA pattern was the basis for the pattern but found what she says may be the original inspiration for that pattern. It is a design by Michelangelo for a continuous pathway in a quadrangle of the Capitol, Rome, shown in an engraving by Du Pirac in 1569. The design is shown in *Celtic Art* by George Bain, published by Dover Press.

FAN, 1976, 81″ x 100″. Made by Nora Mills Reeder. Owned by Ruth Reeder Brill.

RAIL FENCE, 1975, 79″ x 96″. Made and owned by Ruby Reeder Murray.

NOSEGAY, 1977, 81″ x 100″. Made and owned by Ruth Reeder Brill.

KALEIDOSCOPE, 1979, 80″ x 98″. Made and owned by Ruth Reeder Brill.

Another of Averil and Ruth's projects was recreating a quilt from a DOVE IN THE WINDOW quilt that had been made by Ruth's Grandma Mills. They copied a pattern from the quilt and decided not to look at each other's work until they were finished. Their quilts and the original are pictured as part of an article, "Another World in Illinois," about Illinois quilters in the Winter, 1982 issue of *Lady's Circle Patchwork Quilts*.

The Webb sisters of Benton are also mentioned in that article. Quilting has been a family project for Mary, Leotris and Nancy, too. Mary, a high school home economics teacher and Leotris, a first grade teacher, are now retired. Leotris often chose themes that would appeal to her pupils such as CHICKEN LITTLE and PINKY MARIE. She named one of her wallhangings after a doll she kept in her classroom for many years.

The SEA FEATHER quilt is one of their joint projects. They copied the pattern from an old family quilt. Mary said her grandmother, Nancy Jane Britton Webb gave each of her sons a SEA FEATHER quilt. Mary's mother, Lillis Leona Scribner Webb gave her son such a quilt also. The sisters decided to make another one. Mary and Leotris did the applique and all of them quilted it.

SEA FEATHER, 1979, 86″ x 96″. Made by Mary and Leotris Webb, quilted by Nancy, Mary and Leotris Webb. Owned by Mary and Leotris Webb.

Mary still has the LOLLIPOP wallhanging made by Nancy, now deceased and Leotris gave the PINEAPPLE quilt that she pieced to her doctor, James Durham. Their work displays careful stitching, exuberant colors and personal design touches throughout.

Marlene Bennett Webb, their niece, has learned from them as she watched them enjoy and plan their projects. They extend themselves to do their best and pay close attention to detail. Marlene quilted with her grandmother and includes quilted works along with her other work as an artist. Her works in watercolor, acrylics and textile are shown at her Local Artists Gallery in Ewing. Her wall piece called WINDMILLS was done as the result of classwork with quilt artist Nancy Crow at a local community college.

LOLLIPOP, 1979, 43″ x 56″. Made by Nancy Webb. Owned by Mary and Leotris Webb.

PINEAPPLE, 1981, 96″ x 102″. Made by Leotris Webb. Owned by Dr. James P. Durham.

WINDMILLS, 1985, 36″ x 36″. Made and owned by Marlene Webb.

Anna Karg Green of Alton is part of a family group of quilters. Anna, a widow, has helped seven children through college. Along with quilting for herself and others, she has a cake decorating business and is an Avon distributor. She worked on her first quilt by age 15, her effort proving fruitful. Her first quilt deteriorated long ago. She does all types of quilting, patchwork, applique and embroidery. She made quilts with an eagle motif for her four grandsons when each of them was old enough to have a regular size bed.

Frances Karg, Anna's mother, recently gave Anna a quilt that had belonged to her great-grandmother, Josephine Etienne. Josephine came to live near Coulterville from New Orleans. Her family had come to New Orleans from France. The quilt is called the RED ROSE quilt by family members and is at least one hundred and five years old. The basket is pieced of red and green. A red rose is appliqued to the block and cut away to show white areas that form the detail of the bloom, a form of reverse applique. It has the original binding and apparently was a "special" quilt for it does not show much wear.

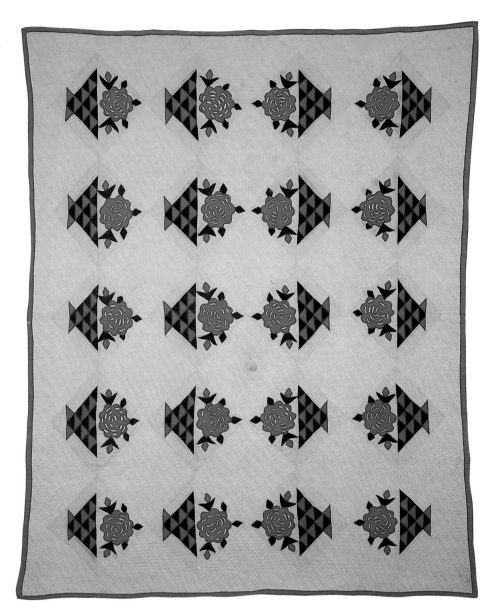

**RED ROSE, Circa 1870, 76" x 86".
Attributed to Josephine Etienne.
Owned by Anna Karg Green.**

Catherine Palcis of Romeoville watched many of the women in her family quilt. She recently completed her first quilt, a LOG CABIN. Her mother, Maxine Evans Palcis has been quilting for many years. She holds a full-time job but has managed to make many items as gifts. She has finished two full-sized bed quilts recently. An all-white quilt features the outlines of hands and feet of family members along with their names.

Maxine said her mother, Mildred Mitchell Evans, who went to work during World War II as a clerk for Illinois Bell, was constantly doing some kind of needlework. Mildred quilted all the time and made each of her grandchildren three quilts. Maxine remembers her favorite grandmother, Rosa Ashbaugh Mitchell as "a tough act to follow." A very resourceful woman, she made everything from doll clothes to wedding dresses and of course, quilts. Rosa's mother, Clara Ashbaugh had come to Illinois by stagecoach and lived at Steger near Chicago Heights.

The MORNING GLORY quilt shown is made from a kit. There is also a blue one still in the family. This quilt represents the work of four generations. Rosa appliqued the blocks 25 to 30 years ago. Since the blocks were all that Maxine got from Rosa, she chose a small floral print for the sashing. Maxine and Catherine used morning glory motifs from several sources to form the quilting design. They quilted the quilt together. Maxine's mother also got to quilt one of the blocks. They consider the quilt their special tribute to a special woman.

MORNING GLORY, 1985, 86″ x 100″. Made by Rosa Ashbaugh Mitchell, Mildred Mitchell Evans, Maxine Evans Palcis and Catherine Palcis. Owned by Maxine Evans Palcis.

Another family project is the ILLINOIS quilt. Shawn Green's parents, Harold and Georgia had placed an Illinois map in their son's room. They kept track of places they had been and places they were to visit on the map. Shawn suggested a quilt based on the map. Georgia said all the family members helped gather information and contributed to the quilt. Some of the fabric came from Shawn's great-grandmother, Lucy Snow Baker. The quilt has been exhibited at Postville, New Salem State Park, the Logan County Fair, the Illinois State Fair and at several events for the Lincoln/Logan County Crafts Guild. Quilting motifs include corn, barnyard and farm scenes and Lincoln's head.

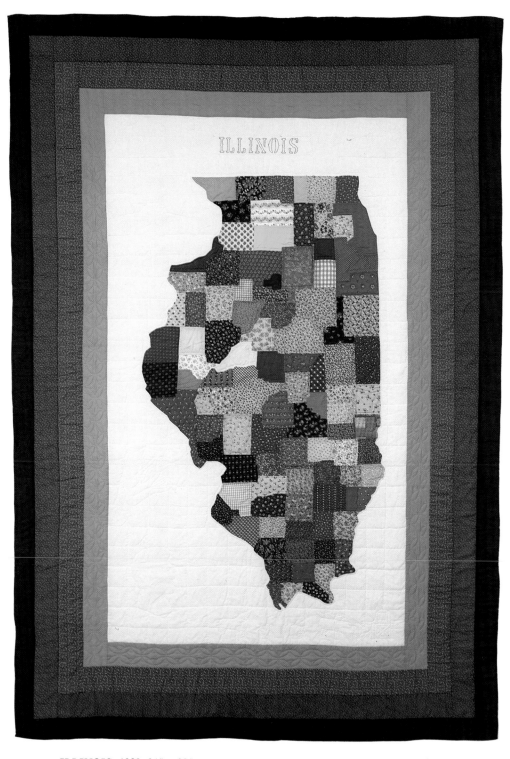

ILLINOIS, 1982, 64″ x 92″. Made by Georgia Green. Owned by Shawn Green.

Quilts form a part of family tradition in many ways. Quilts were made from bits of family clothes or the cloth from which such clothes were cut so that good fabric would not be wasted. Quilts were made to use because they were needed or for occasions special to family members. Quilting was "women's work." The collection of quilts at the Iroquis County Historical Society documents the heritage of quilting in that area. The tradition continues with many area women quilting.

Nancy Crow has quite a collection of quilts from her mother's family. Her mother, grandmother and her grandmother's sister all quilted together at the "home place" in Ohio. Nancy brought quilting skills with her to Illinois. She still quilts at Milford at the age of 92. Her latest piece, a lap quilt, has six-pointed stars just three inches across.

Quilts form a part of community tradition as well. Women still gather to quilt for the benefit of the community and to recognize community occasions. The women of the Milford Junior Women's Club designed a quilt to commemorate Milford's sesquicentennial in 1980. Three community women, Dorothy Wilcox, Maude Hartman and Helen Crawford, did the embroidery and applique of the blocks. The quilt was set together and pieced by Annis Cheever. Annis has quilted for over half a century. The quilt was raffled and the lucky winner and now owner is Kathy McCann of nearby Stockland. Annis also pieced and quilted the BROKEN STAR quilt shown.

BROKEN STAR, 1933, 70″ x 81″. Made by Annis Cheever. Owned by Mabel Cheever.

Annis quilted for people as do many other women in the area including Minnie Schiewe, Mabel Niebuhr, Helen Bennett, Edna Moser and Bonnie Schroeder. Edna, of Goodwine, quilted the SUNBURST quilt which was pieced and appliqued by her mother, Anna Moser, about 1945. It is one of a pair. Edna creates wall hangings and Hawaiian quilts which she exhibits and sells.

SUNBURST, 1945, 74″ x 86″. Pieced and appliqued by Anna Moser, quilted by Edna Moser. Owned by Edna Moser.

Bonnie Schroeder lives at Woodland, near Watseka in Iroquois County. She has quilted since her early twenties and had three finished before her marriage. She has made three quilts for each of her three children and for her grandchildren. Bonnie quilts with other women at St. John's Lutheran Church located at Schwer. They produced a quilt to mark the church's centennial. The quilting at the church started with the Ladies Aid group over sixty-one years ago. The efforts of the group over the years have provided maintenance funds, rugs and a piano for the church. In addition, they have donated to a retarded children's group and Lutheran nursing homes.

Bonnie has quilted for many of the women in the area. She quilted the CRAZY ANN quilt owned by Anise Boyd of Milford. The quilt was pieced by Anise's mother-in-law, Annie D. Boyd. It was made in 1950 from sample pieces of Waverly decorator fabrics which she had collected. Bonnie is a quilt researcher's delight. She has an album with photos of almost every quilt she has made and quilted. It is all neatly labeled with the date and owner and other pertinent information.

CRAZY ANN, 1950, 73″ x 84″. Pieced by Annie D. Boyd, quilted by Bonnie Schroeder. Owned by Anise Boyd.

Another of the quilts that she quilted is the unnamed red geometric quilt owned by Doris O'Neill of Ashkum. The quilt was pieced by Laura Collins Brooks. She was Doris's "step-grandmother." Laura was from an aristocratic English family that lived in Ohio. Her family was involved with the underground railroad during the Civil War. She was a master of many types of needlework and gave Doris many lovely things for her wedding. Doris said of Laura, "She was as dear to me as a blood grandmother could have been, and was happy to introduce me as her granddaughter. Our deep love was mutual. When Laura passed on, the Brooks family had her buried beside my grandfather, his first wife (my real grandmother) on one side and Laura on the other, so he rests between them . . . just family love for Laura . . ."

UNNAMED RED GEOMETRIC, 1935, 76″ x 103″. Pieced by Laura Collins Brooks, quilted by Bonnie Schroeder. Owned by Doris O'Neil.

In Donovan, Carolyn Lindgren, known as "Cad" to friends, is another who quilts for others as well as herself. Now seventy-two, she figures she has been quilting for other people for at least twenty of the more than forty years she has been quilting. She has kept a pictorial record of her work. Carolyn has also been involved with church quilting and remembers the group charging a penny per yard of quilting thread used. She quilts on frames that belonged to her husband's mother.

One of the quilts that she helped to quilt belonged to a friend, Jean Tebo. The quilt which Jean designed is called PINE TREE. Carolyn said it took 35 pairs of hands a little over two weeks to finish. Carolyn asked for help because the quilt was dark. A covered-dish dinner gave the work the feel of an old-time quilting bee. She said they had a great time. In a letter, Carolyn said, "I am 72 years young, keep trying to do what we've always done but there are days . . .''

PINE TREE, 1984, 88″ x 93″. Made by Jean Tebo, quilted by Carolyn Lindgren and friends. Owned by Jean Tebo.

Jean Tebo borrowed the idea for her quilt from another quilt which had been made by her husband's grandmother. Roger remembers his grandmother, Ettie Ellen Brees (1863-1950), as an extremely industrious woman. At the age of 65, she milked the cows without using a stool because she had a bad hip. With the use of a cane, she continued to garden. He remembered radishes from the garden of raised beds that were kept as neat as the many quilts she made.

He has several of the quilts including the one they refer to as the PINE TREE. The quilt is done in dark maroon fabrics with tiny white prints and muslin. The maroon has faded onto the muslin giving it the palest hint of pink. Close scrutiny reveals three mispieced blocks. Whether intentional or error, only Ettie knows.

PINE TREE, Circa 1900, 66″ x 77″. Made by Ettie Ellen Brees. Owned by Roger and Jean Tebo.

Laura and Alice Callahan are sisters-in-law. Married to brothers, Floyd and Elmer Callahan of Milford, both women have quilts from the Callahan family. Their quilting is mostly for their own families. Laura favors embroidery for her quilts and Alice enjoys pieced quilts.

After she opened the door to let me in and introductions had been made, Alice Norton Callahan said, "Now Mrs. Barber, I want you to know I'm happy to show you my quilts, but I want you to

remember - quilts are like hankies, some are for show and some are for blow. And mine are for blow."

The quilts and their stories were as interesting as her opening remark. She had several--some from family and some she'd made herself.

Her CROSS PURPOSES quilt was made in 1950. Another quilt included in the pattern from a Mountain Mist quilt batt wrapper is BOSTON COMMONS. She had most of that quilt pieced but never set it together. She has the fabric to finish it soon.

CROSS PURPOSES, 1950, 75″ x 82″. Made and owned by Alice Callahan.

While showing the quilts, she recalled a story from her childhood. When she was about six years old, she played hooky from school to play with the baby. Together they stood on the porch and watched a storm approach the house. The storm became a tornado which destroyed a nearby church and then caved in her grandparents' house. Her Aunt Dorie's head was cut but there were no other injuries to family members. Neighbors had gone to the grand-

parents' house and taken shelter behind the woodpile. They later told stories of feathers blown off chickens and collars blown off the horses without the harness being unbuckled. A quilt that her great-grandmother had made for her grandmother was found several miles away, entangled in a barbed wire fence. The quilt was brought home, patched, washed and returned to use. It is still in the family.

Virginia Piland of Palatine came to Illinois ten years ago when her husband was transferred. She had never seen her mother or grandmother quilt. They were weavers, as is Virginia. She had been looking for a loom when she became involved in quilting. Her sister was working on a quilt and Virginia thought it looked interesting. "Just kind of fell into it," she said.

Although she never saw her grandmother make bed quilts, Virginia does have a bed that belonged to her. Her grandmother was a schoolmarm in Kentucky. It was the custom of the time for the schoolmarm to "board around" – that is to stay with various families of the community. Room to sleep was not necessarily a problem for the host family, but an extra bed was. So in addition to her teaching skills and a horse to get her around, it was necessary for the schoolmarm to have her own bed. The horse

died. Virginia inherited the bed. She keeps her own quilts on it.

Virginia is a junior high school English teacher. Perhaps it is her long involvement with the written word that makes her work uniquely her own. She considers quilting a dialogue between generations. She feels that what she says with her quilts is more than her words can say.

Her daughters agree with her. Tracy said, "When I see the quilt she made me, it makes me want to write home. I think of love and all the hard work she did for me." She is sure that the quilt gets special care. The SNOWFLAKES quilt was made for daughter Lindsey Piland Vogt. Lindsey knew the quilt was being made but did not go into the room where the work was being done. She wanted to be surprised. When she did see it, she told Virginia, "I didn't know you loved me that much."

SNOWFLAKES, 1981, 96″ x 108″. **Made by Virginia Piland. Owned by Lindsey Piland Vogt.**

When Virginia says, "That's what a quilt does. It talks," she is quite serious. And some of her quilts do "talk." They communicate via words as well as image. Her piece entitled, IT'S TIT FOR TAT RALPH LAUREN has several messages embroidered on it. The wall piece was constructed as a rebuke to fashion designer, Ralph Lauren, who was featuring designer clothing cut from antique quilts. Virginia's quilt is constructed from a Ralph Lauren shirt. It reads as follows:

Around the border:

"It's tit for tat Ralph Lauren. Take that! And that and that and that and that! As you sew so shall you rip, but please Ralph Lauren, don't rip up any more antique quilts. Quilters are sew-super, but Ralph Lauren you are just an old sew and sew. Sew long Ralph Lauren. It's been good to no-no you. Virginia Piland"

On the tie streamers:

"You have been found 'quilt-y'." "You have been sentenced to a stretch on the quilting frame."

On the collar:

"We have collared you."

The pockets of the shirt are labeled, "pins" and "needles" and have small cross-stitch dolls attached "for needling."

TIT FOR TAT, RALPH LAUREN, 1983, 45″ x 45″. Made and owned by Virginia Piland.

The other wall piece is one to which many of us can relate. She found a scarf which was printed with little red-roofed houses and cherry trees. She added several borders with an inscription on the outer one that reads:

"I hate it! I hate it when somebody says to me... ...'You can't possibly miss it, Virginia dear,' 'Go north, go west, turn right, turn left to the little white house with a red-red roof beside a cherry tree.' 'Ginny you ninny you missed it! You missed it!' cried she."

Virginia considers quilting a quiet therapy – but it isn't quiet at a quilt show when people read her quilts. But then, laughter is therapeutic too. Another of her bed quilts called SUDDENLY IT'S SPRING is shown in the *Quilt Art '85 Engagement Calendar* published by the American Quilter's Society. Her major project for the future is a series of wall quilts to depict the epic story of Gilgamesh. Teaching is her vocation; she considers her quilting an avocation.

YOU CAN'T MISS IT, VIRGINIA DEAR, 1984, 25″ x 25″. Made and owned by Virginia Piland.

Another quilter who considers quilting her avocation is Nancy Pearson of Morton Grove. A graphic artist who received her training at the American Academy of Arts and the School of the Art Institute of Chicago, Nancy started quilting in 1975. As a child she had been taught embroidery by her father. She found quilting to be a way to occupy time during a long illness of her daughter. She became serious about the quilting in 1981 and took some workshops and classes.

An instructor for three years, Nancy teaches classes, mostly in applique, judges shows and designs and markets a series of patterns for applique. Her patterns are for the more advanced applique artist. She does not plan to become heavily involved in the business of marketing patterns since her first priority is "to stitch." She said, "I caught the bug so late in life that I'd better hurry up and quilt. Applique is slow. My quilts are the only legacy I have for my family. I hope they will appreciate them." She prefers the traditional type of quilting although she appreciates and is comfortable with modern quilting as well. "There is room for all of us," she said.

Her greatest concern is that craftsmanship be improved. She thinks that some people feel the quilt is done when the top is pieced and so do not put a great deal of quilting into the work. She says, "Applique is like playing a violin--it takes years to do it well. The same is true for good quilting."

Nancy's work is shown on the cover of the April 1985 issue of *Quilter's Newsletter*. The issue contains a brief article about her and her work. In 1984, Nancy entered the juried show, "Quilts: All American Beauty" held by the South/Southwest Quilt Association (now American/International Quilt Association) at their annual Quilt Festival in Houston, Texas. She won five ribbons. Her TECHNY CHIMES quilt was named Best of Show-Artisan and 2nd Place Applique. FAN AND FLORAL won 1st Place Applique and her NANCY'S GARDEN won both the Founder's Choice and a Judge's Choice Award. It was the first juried show she had ever entered. She was glad she did.

NANCY'S GARDEN.

Nancy Pearson gives her friend Rita Runquist credit for helping her get more involved in the business world of quilting. Rita gave her encouragement and put her in contact with other quilt business people.

Rita Runquist of Cary is much involved in quilting herself. She sells many of her projects and does commission work in addition to quilting for herself. An interesting aspect of her involvement is organizing tours for quilting groups.

The tours sound exciting. Rita uses her creative mind to put together an itinerary that includes not just quilt shops and shows, but other items of interest in whatever area they happen to be visiting on a particular tour. One of the activities of the tours is participating in a fabric co-op. Each participant contributes money to a "pool" which is used to purchase fabrics. At the end of the tour the fabrics are divided so that each participant gets a section of all the fabrics purchased. Can you imagine a group of avid quilters sitting up 'til the wee hours of the morning cutting and folding fabric to be shared? It sounds like a marvelous way to gather fabrics for scrap or charm quilts. It also sounds like a "fabricholic's" idea of heaven.

One of the favorite stops for Rita's tours is the shop of Sara Miller in Kalona, Iowa. Kalona Kountry Kreations features hundreds of bolts of fabrics and on some occasions dinner for the group is prepared by Sara. Having the kind of selection by shops like Sara's is important to Rita. She is particularly fond of scrap quilts. Her BLUE SCRAP is shown. It has over eighty different blue prints in it. In addition to the constant search for new fabrics to use in her quilts, Rita looks forward to exploring new ideas with design and color in her future work.

BLUE SCRAP, 1980, 82″ x 96″. Made and owned by Rita Runquist.

Rita's grandmother, Mary Sinclair made many scrap quilts. Rita remembers her having a pillowcase full of piecing that she would get out each day during the Art Linkletter radio show. All of Mary's quilts were scraps combined with muslin or plain white fabric, but Rita said some of them were very intricate patterns with many curves. During her college days, Rita used quilts that Mary made. She still has them. "I wish I could tell her now how much more I appreciate her work. She would be pleased that quilts are gaining so much respect," Rita said.

Marion L. Huyck of Evanston is another urban quilter along with Virginia Piland, Nancy Pearson, Rita Runquist and many others who defy the stereotypic image of a quilter as a little old woman in the country. Marion describes herself as being on the "art end" of quilting in that she makes quilts more for decorative purposes than utilitarian ones. She said she makes quilts because she absolutely loves the process of it. Once it's made, she doesn't particularly care to have them all around--she's ready to move on to another.

Her direct involvement with quilting came as the result of attending a mini-class offered between terms at the school in which she taught. Although she had been familiar with patchwork, the class was her first experience at the actual process. After the two-day class, she proceeded to make her first quilt.

Her grandmother had quilted, but Marion never saw the work until after her death. After she started quilting, her grandfather gave her a box that had been her grandmother's. The box contained newspaper clippings that may have been part of the original McKim series of patterns in addition to blocks, unsewn cut pieces and other things. She later received two quilts that had been made by a great-grandmother.

In addition to her quilting, Marion teaches in area quilt shops. As a teacher, she wishes to help her students acquire a sense of "self". As a quilt artist, she wants to bring pleasure with her work. When asked what sort of quilts attract her attention she said, "Quilts that demand a second look . . . the way color is used . . . the way the design works . . . something in the piece that teases you." Those phrases could be used to describe her work as well.

Her piece entitled RUSSIAN MEDALLION was inspired by the work of a Russian graphic artist, Ivan Bilibin, who died in 1919. He, in turn was inspired by Russian folk art. Bilibin illustrated several series of Russian fairy tales. She said of the piece, "I often work in the medallion style, perhaps because I am always trying for a central focus in my own life. I also love borders, not just on quilts, but particularly border gardens, the edges of things, architectural detailing on buildings. This quilt celebrates borders and color." The quilt is both pieced and appliqued in all cotton fabrics and hand quilted.

RUSSIAN MEDALLION. Made and owned by Marion L. Huyck.

Marion hopes to see more art quilts in galleries and more exhibits of modern contemporary quilts. She would like to see quilts taken more seriously by the academic art community as original work.

A background in the art world formed the basis for Millie Dunkel's work in quilting. Although her early work emphasized painting and sculpture, she started working with fibers. She moved from dyeing fabric to batiking, then incorporated quilting to add dimension to the work. She has worked on commission for the last three years.

Millie likes to think of wall quilts as paintings with the quilting line acting as a drawing line. While she has no trouble considering quilting an art form, she also likes to do practical things like bed quilts. She describes herself as fascinated with the history of quilts and the women who made them.

BABY ANIMALS, 1979. Made and owned by Millie Dunkel.

Two pieces of Millie's work are shown, both feature batiking as a method of giving design to the fabric. The HEARTS AND HANDS quilt has a special story. It was made following the death of one of her sons. The hands were patterned from the hands of people special to her, the border is cherubs with wings. An inscription on the quilt reads, "This quilt is my comforter . . . made in honor of my dear friends . . . who over the years have handed me their hearts. Millie Dunkel 1979."

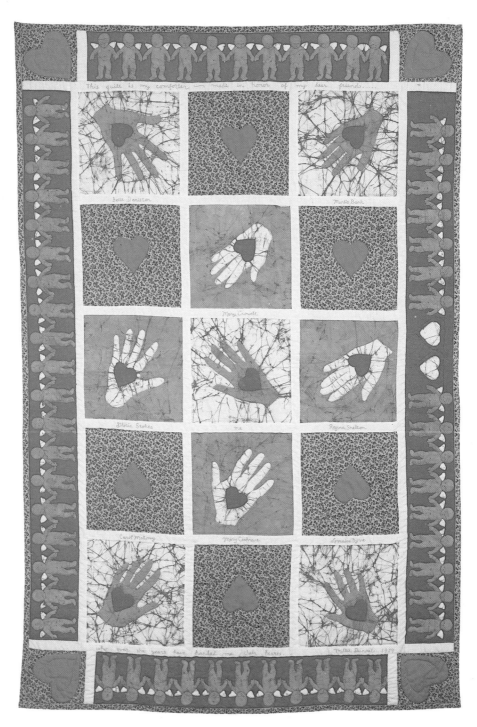

HEARTS AND HANDS, 1979. Made and owned by Millie Dunkel.

In addition to her own work, Millie involved herself in a community project. She had the idea for a quilt as a result of a tour of historical houses in Carbondale. The idea lay dormant until a new public library was being planned. Millie felt the library would be a good home for such a quilt. Several other local artists and craftswomen were "called and some threatened" as Millie put it. With donated materials and time, they created a commemorative quilt that was hung in time for the opening of the new building in July of 1983.

CARBONDALE COMMEMORATIVE, 1983, 80″ x 102″. Cooperative effort of local artists and craftswomen, headed by Millie Dunkel.

One of the participating artists in the Carbondale commemorative quilt project was Carolyn DeHoff. An art teacher who has always sewn and is a weaver as well, describes herself as having "a lifelong affinity for fiber and fabric." Since she became involved in quilting in 1977, Carolyn has taken classes with Chris Wolf Edmonds, Michael James and Nancy Crow. The piece shown was begun during a workshop with Nancy Crow.

Carolyn now focuses on the design and piecing of her quilts and has the quilting done. She still designs the quilting pattern as well. She has been working with a Japanese technique called "shibori" which involves first tying and then dyeing the fabric before using it.

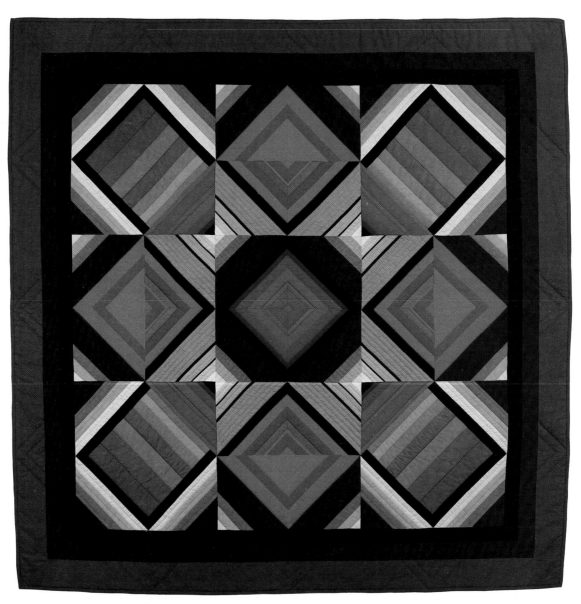

UNNAMED, 1984, 56" x 56". Made and owned by Carolyn DeHoff.

Graphic artist Martha Pooley of Edwardsville describes her work with quilting and other media as a way of filling the need to be creative. It takes her away from the commercial design projects involving her job with a local print shop. She likes being able to create exactly what she wants – to have something "I've created."

The piece shown is unnamed. "I've kept trying to come up with a version of KING TUTANKHAMEN but just never got it re-arranged to suit me," she said. "Joe just didn't seem to fit." (Joe is the name of one of Martha's cats.) Martha first did the design that she has used in her wall quilt in wood and metal. It is one of the designs that she has included in her recently published, *Catalog*. An idea book for cat lovers, the book features designs of cats which can be adapted for woodwork, needlework, stained glass and other arts and crafts. She is anxious to see how others interpret her design ideas.

UNNAMED, 1984, 45″ x 56″. Made and owned by Martha Pooley.

Edward Larsen of Libertyville is another artist who adopted quilting after working with other art forms. He had taught at the Art Institute of Chicago for several years and wanted to get away from the city. His search for another area in which to work brought him into contact with quilters in southern Missouri where he was reared. For a time he was involved in buying and selling quilts he found in the area.

He tells the story of going to visit his mother and having several quilts with him. He was particularly fond of one of them so he put it on the bed in the room which he was using. When he returned to the room later in the day, it was gone. He asked his mother what had become of the quilt. She had put it in the closet. He returned it to his bed. It disappeared again the next day. Further inquiry into the matter revealed his mother's attitude regarding quilts. She had been raised in the country and felt that as soon as possible one got "store-bought" things for the house. She felt the quilt did not belong in her well-kept house.

Ed's work with quilting involves partnerships with quilters who are willing to work with him in creating a quilt which he has designed. In this way, he combines his strength in designing with the quilter's strength in technique and fabric selection. His quilts are pictorial in nature, showing scenes which represent things important in the lives of the people he represents. They are often personal and humorous. He started working on this kind of quilt because there are so few in the public domain. He feels this type of quilt tells the viewer about many dimensions of the designer and quilter. The idea expressed in the quilt takes on new dimension as well when it is transferred from him to quilter and fabric.

Ed has participated in the prestigious fashion show produced for several years by Fairfield Processing Corporation. Each year as many as fifty artists are invited to submit a garment for the show. The garments include techniques in quilting design and construction. Ed's garment featured Annie Oakley and was included in the 1984 show. It was constructed by Ohio quilt artist Fran Soika.

He has done commission quilts for companies such as Quaker Oats and Household Finance. Some of the people featured in his quilts are Big Bill Haywood, Muhammad Ali, Jesse Jackson, Martin Luther King Jr., Sally Rand, Abraham Lincoln and George Washington. Ed enjoys workshops where he can help people create their own quilt experience.

ANNIE OAKLEY, 1984. Designed by Edward Larson. Constructed by Fran Soika.

Ed designed the WASHINGTON ISLAND quilt shown. He has often worked on Washington Island and his work is frequently displayed in a gallery there. The quilt was constructed by another Illinoisian, Cathy Grafton. She spent eight months of 1983 (450 hours) working on the quilt. It has been shown at the 1983 Wisconsin Quilters Fall Symposium and at the Zolla Liberman Gallery in Chicago.

Cathy, who also writes and teaches in addition to her quilting, lives in Pontiac. She is currently working on a series of PRAIRIE QUILTS which will depict colors and scenes of Illinois prairie land near her home. Ed Larson has designed one of the quilts in the series. The quilts will be the basis of her next series of lectures and workshops. She has taught miniature quiltmaking for the last three years. Her work has led to a strong interest in quilt preservation and history as well.

WASHINGTON ISLAND, 1983. Designed by Edward Larson. Constructed by Cathy Grafton.

Russell Sherman of Quincy has been involved with needlework in one form or another since he was eight years old. He has done embroidery, crochet and needlepoint. Several quilt tops are part of his embroidery work. He also has created an applique quilt; someone else did the quilting.

Russ has worked on other quilts as well. He and his wife, Esther, have an antique shop, Sherman's Antiques, which she manages. Quilts are brought to them or they get them at auctions and estate sales. His daughter, Sheila, had always wanted a FLOWER GARDEN quilt. They found an unfinished one at an auction. An unfinished TRIP AROUND THE WORLD was purchased at the same time. The pieces are barely an inch across in each quilt. The boxes in which they were found had the partially-finished tops, cut pieces strung together ready to be pieced, pattern pieces and charts for the layout. After trying for some time to find someone willing to finish the quilts, he ended up doing them himself. They all worked at figuring out the layout. Finishing the FLOWER GARDEN was his first real experience with patchwork. He gave the much desired quilt to Sheila.

A few years ago, he saw a CRAZY QUILT at a Quincy quilt show. It intrigued him. He began collecting fabrics and old men's ties to use in such a quilt. His CRAZY QUILT is shown. Russ has given the quilt to his daughter Sheila and is making another for daughter Nancy. "With two daughters I'm busy trying to keep them both happy," he said. "They never really say, 'I want that quilt.' Instead they'll ask, 'What are you going to do with that one?'"

It would be possible to study the CRAZY QUILT for hours and never really see all that is in it. Besides the many different fabrics, there are well over seventy different embroidery stitches or techniques, some small appliques and stuffed work. One block has an inscription, "To Sheila, R. Sherman." Transfer designs for some of the embroidery motifs date back to the early 1900's.

CRAZY QUILT, 86″ x 96″. Made by Russell Sherman. Owned by Sheila Sherman.

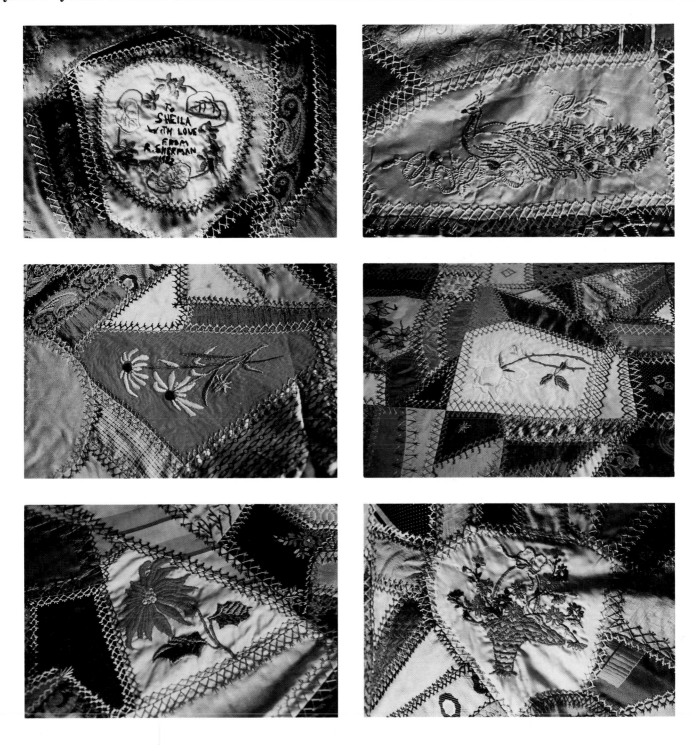

Russ looks forward to his needlework as a means of relaxation from the stress of his busy job as an international buyer for a corporation. Russ and a friend were the local quilting teacher's first male students. She was undoubtedly happy to learn he won a ribbon at a county fair for one of his quilts. He does not find that men react negatively to his needlework. As a matter of fact a friend, also male, has helped solve his problem of finding a thimble to fit. With that equipment now available, he is ready to learn to do his own quilting. Having learned techniques and fabric selection, he is ready to move into more creative aspects of quilting. He has several designs on paper.

Russell Sherman and Charles Stinson have several things in common although they have never met. Charles and his wife, Betty, own an antique shop in Kankakee – Bellflower Antiques. Charles has made quilts too. His first experience with quilting came as a child of eight. His mother gave him patches to make into blocks during an illness, a quiet occupation for an ailing youngster. She completed the quilt. Charles still has the simple nine-patch. In 1948 he made another quilt based on the nine-patch design which he designed and called LEADED GLASS WINDOW.

Charles Stinson pictured with his LEADED GLASS WINDOW.

The quilt shown is now called CALICO FAN-TASY. When he made it in 1947, he and his family referred to it as CHARLIE'S BRAINSTORM. Charles took his design inspiration from an 1890 English fireplace tile. He constructed the quilt of fabrics collected over a period of many years from auctions. The original design features piecing and applique. He had the quilting done. Charles said he looked a long time for just the right stripe to use as the border for the piece. He finally ended up using the stripes cut from fabric that had been meant for a sling-type lawn chair. The quilt was made during a time when Charles first came to Kankakee to work before his family could join him.

Charles is no longer quilting but is president of the Kankakee County Historical Society. He has been active in sponsoring many interesting exhibits featuring quilts from the society's collection. The collection includes many quilts of particular interest in the history of the area.

CALICO FANTASY, 1947, 88″ x 102″. Made and owned by Charles Stinson.

Historians and Collectors

Richard Raymond of Springfield works at the Lincoln Home Historical Site. Part of his work revolves around the collection of textiles including quilts that are featured at the site. Richard has studied textiles in France and Canada as well as in the United States. He is a practicing textile artist who came from a quilting family. He remembers his grandparents both as quilters and said his grandfather was meticulous in his work.

He started collecting with a LOG CABIN quilt for which he paid $7.00 and that included documentation. Richard chooses pieces for his collection which he considers exceptional either graphically or in workmanship. One of his favorites is the AMISH BARS shown. The quilting design is in diagonal rows on the red and green bars and in overlapping waves or shells on the ivory bars. He said it reminds him of rows in the fields and clouds.

AMISH BARS, 70″ x 84″. Date and maker unknown. Owned by Richard Raymond.

People who work with textiles as a profession are important to the preservation and conservation of our textile heritage. We tend to take textiles for granted because they are such an integral part of our everyday environment. Some people, like Richard Raymond or Olivia Mahoney of the Chicago Historical Society, work with public institutions to manage their textile collections which often include quilts. In addition to preserving special quilts, these collections are important to our culture as a resource for reference and study.

Other people are also important to the preservation of textiles, particularly quilts. This group includes those who are dealers and/or collectors. Jean Shelor Lyle of Quincy is one of this group. She has been involved as a dealer and collector for nearly fifteen years. For the last eight years, she has been attending shows as a dealer in pre-1940 quilts.

Jean is as enthused about the people she meets as she is about finding new quilts. She takes the time to talk with the people to find out as much as possible about each quilt. She accuses herself of being real picky about selling her quilts. She once refused to sell a quilt to a woman who said she was going to cut it up to make stuffed animals. She later sold the quilt to a woman who described it as just perfect for a brick wall in her family room. Jean said it came as quite a shock to see the quilt (on the brick wall the woman had described) featured in a national decorating magazine. She is glad the quilt found a home where it was cherished.

Her favorite story about finding a quilt is about a woman who was delighted to show her quilts and talk about them but not particularly willing to sell any. When Jean and the woman talked, the woman was working on a OCEAN WAVE quilt. The quilt was intended for her son. Several months later Jean received a call from the woman who asked her to come back, she was ready to sell some quilts. When Jean arrived she saw the OCEAN WAVE. She asked why the woman was now going to sell the quilt that had been intended for her son. The reply: "I gave him and his wife the quilt and when I went to visit, the dog was using it for a bed. I decided I'd rather have my quilts go to someone who appreciated them."

Two quilts that Jean has found very special are shown. The TARGET quilt (also called BULLSEYE) came from southeast Iowa. The quilt, which was never finished, was made by a Methodist church sewing group as a fund-raising project. The fabrics had been donated to the church. Each block is composed of hundreds of small circles folded into fourths and then sewn to a foundation piece of fabric in concentric circles. It is quite heavy. She purchased the quilt from another dealer who had bought it at a yard sale.

TARGET or BULLSEYE, Circa 1920, 70″ x 70″. Made by a Methodist church women's group. Owned by Jean Shelor Lyle.

Jean has only seen two other quilts like this one. One was in a shop in Texas and had been used as a rug. The other was shown in the December, 1976 issue of *Quilter's Newsletter* and is in the collection of Ronald and Marcia Spark of Arizona. A similar quilt is shown in *America's Quilts and Coverlets* by Carleton L. Safford and Robert Bishop. It is called SUNBURST and is made by the same technique.

The TREE OF LIFE quilt is from Nauvoo, Illinois. Nauvoo was settled in 1839 by Mormons who were fleeing religious persecution in Missouri. Mormon is the name given to members of the Church of Jesus Christ of Latter Day Saints. The land located north of Hannibal was marshy and swampy. Malaria dimmed the hope of the new settlers for a safe haven.

Hard work and persistence turned the area from swamp to productive farmland. The story of the Mormons in the city is an interesting one. By 1846 tension between the Mormons and their neighbors had again increased. The Mormons moved further west to the Great Salt Lake Basin in Utah where their creative energy would carve the city of Salt Lake from the desert surroundings.

This quilt is dated 1890 and is initialed above the date, "S.A.," and below it, "McG". The solid blocks between the trees are embroidered with motifs that represent things special to the maker. The motifs include flowers known in the area, a horse, a cat, a bird and human figures.

TREE OF LIFE, 1890, 70″ x 83″. Maker unknown. Owned by Jean Shelor Lyle.

Jane Foley of Arthur is an antique dealer. Her shop, which features a tea room, is called NaNa's Treasures. Quilts are an important part of her inventory. She has a separate room where the unfinished tops are neatly folded in cabinets and the quilts are stacked and draped around the rest of the area. There is a quilt in the frame, too. Often she and her mother, Connie Bowers spend time quilting, sometimes on an old top that "needed to be finished" or on a top that they have made. The shop was mentioned in the Illinois issue of *Lady's Circle Patchwork Quilts*, Winter 1982 edition.

The quilt shown from Jane's collection is a tiny eight-pointed star pattern. Dated and signed, the quilt was made in 1882 by two sisters – Maranda and Martha Price. Martha was 28 years old when the quilt was made. It is presumed the quilt was made for Martha's dowry. She later gave the quilt to her

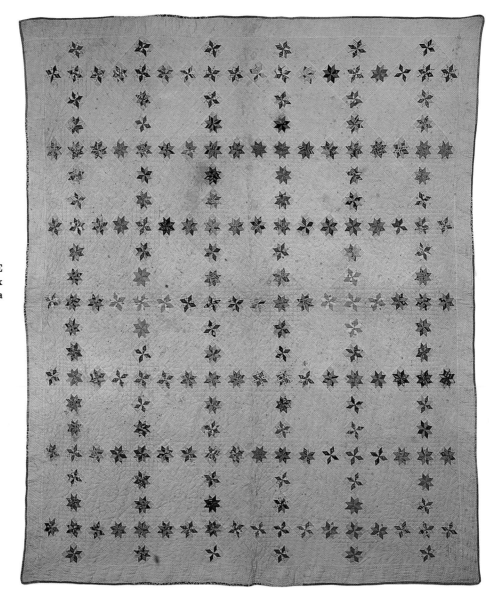

EIGHT-POINTED STAR/NINE PATCH VARIATION, 1882, 66″ x 76″. Made by Maranda and Martha Price. Owned by Jane Foley.

son Martin Wiley Chandler and his wife, Alphea. Alphea loaned the quilt to Ada Jean Kinney who gave quilt programs for organizations. "It was unique and I loved it," says Ada Jean. When Alphea broke up housekeeping, she gave the quilt to Ada Jean, "Because you love it so much." Ada Jean has shown the quilt at the Rockome quilt show where it won Grand Champion/Antique Class. Now that Ada Jean has broken up housekeeping too, she sold the quilt to Jane.

The quilt was pieced as a nine patch, then set together on the bias, giving horizontal rows of little stars and rows straight up and down. Left over fabric from the stars was sewn together for the binding. The quilting is fine and even. In the solid areas the design is a feathered wreath flower with a stem and two leaves extending into one corner and single leaves in the other three corners.

Dorothy Callahan Christian of Watseka is just learning to quilt. But she has been active for several years with the Iroquois County Historical Society Museum. When she retired, she became more involved with the historical society. She has energy enough to keep several people busy. She has seen to it that the quilts are recorded on film. The quilts now have neat muslin bags tagged with identification. Last year she organized a show of quilts from the county; it drew some of the biggest crowds (and donations) of any event held at the museum. Another show is already in the works. It is the interest, energy and dedication of people like Dorothy that keep small museums with volunteer staffs working to preserve the articles, including quilts, that represent our cultural heritage. Like the professionals, volunteers play an important part.

Somewhere In Between

Old quilters-new quilters, craftsperson-artist, dealer-professional-volunteer, all of these people are important to the growing heritage of quilting in Illinois. Like those elsewhere, they are like some other quilters, no other quilters and all other quilters. They share like techniques, unique and original ideas and a strong love of quilts, They recognize and respect the heritage of past quilters, the innovation of present quilters and the ever-increasing interest in quilting now being realized.

The accomplished quilters of Illinois are too numerous to mention at length. Others deserving of recognition include Jennifer Baker of Staunton and her associate, Laurie Mehalko, who design quilts for children and have written a children's quilt book; Margaret Bowman of Oak Park who teaches in the United States and in England and whose ideas seem limitless; June Culvey of Garden Prairie whose exquisite workmanship begs to be admired; Genevieve Bakel of Mt. Vernon who takes tradition and builds upon it; Violet Ebers of Steelville who quilts and manages a quilt museum; Caryl Bryer Fallert of Oswego whose work is winning awards and recognition. All these people have much to share as well. These are only a few of the hundreds who quilt in this state.

Illinois, situated between the East and the West – the North and the South, is both urban and rural.

Between today and tomorrow, Illinois will change with the rest of the world. It's home to many quilters who have grown up here, to new pioneers who have followed work or mates to come and live here.

All of those interviewed for this book expressed many common feelings about this thing called quilting. Warmth that is beyond physical warmth, sharing, satisfaction in creation, in expressing themselves-all of these things have been said. Millie Dunkel may have expressed it best in a letter to me:

"There was a time, after my third or fourth son, that the only creative thing I thought I did was make bread. And as I kneaded the dough on the old kitchen table I felt a certain kinship with the millions of women in the world who were doing the same and it was a good feeling. Likewise with the making of quilts.

Some days when the designing, dyeing and layout work is finished and like today-I sit quietly at my hoop with yards of quilted fabric at one side and yards to go, I feel the same kind of kinship. I know that there are young fingers cautiously practicing those first thousand quilting stitches and beautifully worn old fingers perhaps finishing their last million and hopefully I'm somewhere in between."

Bibliography

Bain, George, *Celtic Art: The Methods of Construction*, New York, Dover Publications, Inc. 1973.

Barr, Thelma, editor, "Marian Brockschmidt", *Patchwork Patter*, Vol. 5 No. 2, Greenbelt, MD, National Quilting Association, May 1977.

Benberry, Cuesta, "The Superb Mrs. Stenge", *Nimble Needle Treasures*, Spring, 1981.

Bishop, Robert, *Knopf Collector's Guide to American Antiques: Quilts, Coverlets, Rugs & Sampler*, New York, Chanticleer Press, Inc., 1982.

Burlend, Rebecca, *A True Picture of Emigration*, edited by Milo Milton Quaife, Chicago, The Lakeside Press, R.R. Donnelley & Sons Co., Christmas 1936.

Cook, Blanche Moye, editor, *History of the Downen Family*, Compiled by the Descendants of Timothey Downen, A.R. Bradley Publishing, 1974.

Gross, Joyce ed., "Bertha Stenge", *Quilter's Journal*, Vol. 3 No. 2, Mill Valley, CA, 1980.

Holstein, Jonathan, *The Pieced Quilt: An American Design Tradition*, Greenwich, CT, New York Graphic Society Ltd., 1973.

Howard, Robert P., *Illinois: A History of the Prairie State*, Grand Rapids, MI, William B. Erdmans Publishing Company, 1972.

Houck, Carter, "Another World in Illinois", *Lady's Circle Patchwork Quilts*, #28, New York, Lopez Publications, Inc., Winter '82-'83.

Leman, Bonnie, "Pictorial Quilts-A New Trend", *Quilter's Newsletter* Magazine, Issue 86, Vol. 7 No 12, Wheatridge, CO, Leman Publications, Inc., December 1976.

Linch-Zadel, Lauri, "The Meetin' Place", *Quilter's Newsletter* Magazine, Issue 171, Vol. 16 No 4, Wheatridge, CO, Leman Publications, Inc., April 1985.

Nelson, Cyril I. and Houck, Carter, *Treasury of American Quilts*, New York, Greenwich House/Crown Publishers, 1982.

McMillion, Betty, "Grandma's House....", *Quilt World*, Vol. 10 No. 1, Seabrook, NH, The House of White Birches, Inc./Tower Press, January/February 1985.

Orlofsky, Patsy and Myron. *Quilts In America*, New York, McGraw-Hill Book Company, 1974.

Reddall, Winifred, "Pieced Lettering on Seven Quilts Dating from 1833 to 1891", *Uncoverings*, Mill Valley, CA, American Quilt Study Guild, 1980.

Safford, Carleton L., and Bishop, Robert, *America's Quilts and Coverlets*, New York, Bonanza, 1985.

Tillson, Christiana Holmes, *A Woman's Story of Pioneer Illinois*, edited by Milo Milton Quaife, The Lakeside Press, Chicago, R.R. Donnelley & Sons Company, Christmas MCMXIX.

American Quilter, Vol. 1, No. 2, Paducah, KY, American Quilter's Society, Fall 1985.

South Carolina Archives, Affidavit re Revolutionary War service of Josiah Downen, Comp. General Accts. Audited for Rev. War Service, AA2014, item #2LL.

200 Years of American Quilts In Illinois Private Collections, Center for Visual Arts Gallery, Illinois State University, Normal, 1976.